ID-UL-FITR

Kerena Marchant

The Millbrook Press
Brookfield, Connecticut

Published by The Millbrook Press
2 Old New Milford Road
Brookfield, Connecticut 06804

Editor: Sarah Doughty
Designer: Tim Mayer

First published in 1996 by Wayland Publishers, Ltd.
61 Western Road, Hove, East Sussex, BN3 1JD

Library of Congress Cataloging-in-Publication Data

Marchant, Kerena.
Id-ul-Fitr / Kerena Marchant.
p. cm — (Festivals)
Includes bibliographical references and index.
Summary: Looks at some of the ways Muslims around the
world celebrate the joyous festival of Id-ul-Fitr.

ISBN 0-7613-0963-2 (lib. bdg.)
1. Id-ul-Fitr—Juvenile literature. 2. Islam—Customs and
practices—Juvenile literature [1. Fasts and feasts—Islam.
2. Fasts and feasts—Islam. 3. Islam—Customs and practices.
4. Holidays.]
I. Title. II. Series
BP186.45.M27 1998
297.36—dc2197-46035
                    CIP
                    AC

Printed and bound by L.E.G.O. S.p.A., Vicenza, Italy

A note on this book:
The symbol ﷺ is used each time the Prophet Muhammad ﷺ is mentioned. It means "Sallallahu alaihi was sallam"(peace and blessings of Allah upon him) and is used to show respect.

A note on dates:
Muslims do not use the Christian calendar. The dates in this book are CE, meaning Common Era.

Picture acknowledgements
Eye Ubiquitous 5 right, 23 bottom; Sally and Richard Greenhill 22, 24; the Hutchison Library (Kerstin Rodgers) 17; Christine Osborne 4 top, middle and bottom left, 5 left, 7 top, 12, 16, 19 (both), 21, 26 (B.Hanson), 27; Peter Sanders title page, 4 bottom right, 6, 7 bottom, 8, 9, 11 (both), 13, 15, 18, 20 (both), 23 top, 28, 29; Trip 10 (Nasa), 25 (F.Good). Islamic typestting on cover by Newlook Translations, border artwork by Tim Mayer.

Permissions
Although the publishers have attempted to contact permission holders, we apologize if we have been unable to contact the owners to secure permissions.

CONTENTS

ID-UL-FITR AROUND THE WORLD

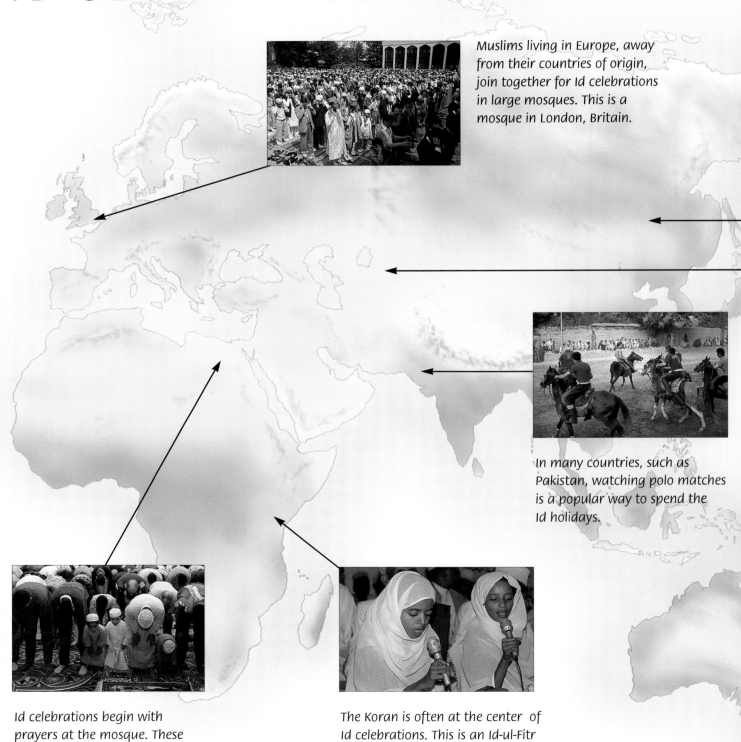

Muslims living in Europe, away from their countries of origin, join together for Id celebrations in large mosques. This is a mosque in London, Britain.

In many countries, such as Pakistan, watching polo matches is a popular way to spend the Id holidays.

Id celebrations begin with prayers at the mosque. These Muslims are in Cairo, Egypt.

The Koran is often at the center of Id celebrations. This is an Id-ul-Fitr Koran reading competition in Kenya, eastern Africa.

Muslims give money to the poor before they begin their Id celebrations. These Muslims live in Lanzhou, China.

In the days leading up to Id, Muslims from Uzbekistan read their holy book, the Koran, from cover to cover.

WHAT IS ID-UL-FITR?

In Arabic, the word "id" means "happiness." Id-ul-Fitr is the most joyous festival in the Muslim calendar. The festival begins after Ramadan, the month when many Muslims fast from sunrise to sunset. Id-ul-Fitr marks the end of Ramadan. Everybody is happy when Ramadan comes to an end and Id-ul-Fitr arrives. It is a great achievement to fast for a month and Id-ul-Fitr celebrates that achievement.

As followers of Islam, Muslims believe that it is important to live good lives and do exactly what Allah (known in many other religions as God) wants them to do. They know how to do this because their holy book, the Koran, tells them what to do.

Part of the Id celebrations is the party atmosphere that takes over after Muslims have prayed at the mosque. This is a celebration in Regent's Park in Britain, with vendors selling delicious food and toys.

ID SONG

"Id has Come" is a folk song that Muslims in India sing at Id. It is sung in Urdu; this is the English translation:

Id has come, Id has come
It makes us happy, it makes us happy
Let's dance and sing, let's dance and sing
Celebrate Id! Celebrate Id!

The festival of Id-ul-Fitr celebrates the fact that Allah gave Muslims the Koran to help them to live good lives. Muslims believe that fasting helps them to think more about Allah and what Allah wants them to do. It also celebrates the good things that come about by fasting. For example, during a fast, a Muslim might decide to change his or her life in different ways—perhaps make up after an argument or help people who are poor. In this way, Id-ul-Fitr is a time of new beginnings, and also a time of peace.

Muslims spend a great deal of time reading their holy books, especially the Koran, so that they can live good lives.

There are both serious and joyous parts to the Id celebrations. When Id arrives, prayers are said at a mosque, usually followed by celebrations with family and friends.

Desserts are prepared for Id to celebrate the end of the month of fasting.

THE PROPHET MUHAMMAD ﷺ FASTS

The word "Islam" means "to submit," and for followers of Islam this means to submit their lives to the will of Allah, and to live their lives according to this will. Early Muslims did this by carefully following instructions given by Prophets like Abraham, Moses, and Jesus. The last of the prophets, and the most important to Muslims, was Muhammad ﷺ and it was through him that the Koran was given.

Muhammad ﷺ was born in 570 CE, in Mecca, which is in present-day Saudi Arabia. Muhammad ﷺ was a member of the Quraysh tribe living in the desert. He loved Allah and spent many hours alone praying, meditating, and fasting. His favorite place was a cave on Mount Hira, just outside Mecca.

One night God sent the angel Gabriel to Muhammad ﷺ. Gabriel saidthat he was to be "the messenger of God" and ordered him to read from a scroll. Muhammad ﷺ explained that he could not read or write and asked Gabriel to recite the words on the scroll for him. Muhammad ﷺ remembered what he had been told and got his secretary, Zaid, to write it down. Muhammad ﷺ preached to other people about what he had been told.

Muslim pilgrims climb to the top of Mount Hira to visit the cave where the angel Gabriel recited the Koran to the Prophet Muhammad ﷺ.

The Arabic word for the Koran is al-Qur'an, which means "to recite." The Koran is the most beautiful Arabic poetry. Being unable to read or write, it is unlikely that Muhammad ﷺ could have written it. This is why Muslims have no difficulty in believing that the messages really did come from Allah.

Muhammad ﷺ made all his followers fast during the month of Ramadan, which is when he received his first visit from Gabriel.

This is a copy of the Koran. The writing is in Arabic. Around the verses the pages are beautifully decorated using colored patterns and paint made from real gold. Pictures are never used because in Islam it is forbidden to draw pictures of people.

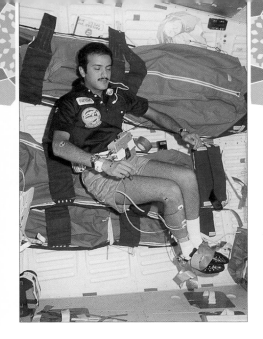

Prince Sultan-bin-Sulman spent Ramadan in a spacecraft. People who go on long journeys can be excused from fasting, but Prince Sultan-bin-Sulman decided to show his love of Allah and devotion to Islam by fasting in space.

The Ramadan fast begins at dawn and ends at sunset. During the hours of fast, nobody eats or drinks anything. In some hot countries, Muslims call Ramadan "the month of thirst" because they have nothing to drink in these hours. In cold countries Muslims suffer hardship because they cannot eat hot food and drink to keep themselves warm. However most Muslims agree that the most difficult place to fast is in non-Muslim countries where everybody else is eating and drinking all the time.

The Prophet Muhammad ﷺ gave his followers clear instructions on how to fast. He suggested that every Muslim should eat a light meal before dawn and drink plenty of water. He also advised Muslims to break their fast with a drink of water and a light meal of three dates at sunset, followed by a bigger meal after prayers. Muslims in different countries have their own traditions of breaking a fast after the Ramadan prayers, but most eat food that is not too rich. There are some people who do not have to fast at all. These include pregnant women, children under twelve, the elderly and sick.

RAMADAN IN SPACE

Nothing will stop Muslims fasting and reading the Koran at Ramadan. Prince Sultan-bin-Sulman, a member of the Saudi royal family, was accepted as an astronaut on an American space mission. The mission was launched during Ramadan and the prince was determined to go to space and to keep Ramadan. Pictures of him at Ramadan were beamed down to Earth.

A Muslim family follows the Prophet's advice and breaks their fast with a light meal of fruit and vegetable pastries and a drink of water.

Throughout Ramadan Muslims recite the Koran. The Koran is divided into thirty equal parts, one for each day of Ramadan. Muslims either recite the Koran to themselves or meet up with friends for group sessions. A special night for Koran reading is called Laylat-ul-Qadr, the Night of Power. This night falls on the 27th night of Ramadan and it is said to be the night when the angel Gabriel first recited the Koran to Muhammad ﷺ on Mount Hira. Throughout this night extra prayers are said and many Muslims stay awake all night reciting the Koran.

Muslims treasure copies of the Koran and copies of it are usually kept on a special stand, so that it does not get torn or worn out.

RAMADAN PRAYERS

Muslims begin their fast at dawn by saying a special prayer:

"O, God, I intend to fast today in obedience to your command and only to seek your pleasure."
Muslims also say a special prayer before they break their fast by eating dates and drinking water:
"O, God! For your sake we have fasted and now we break the fast with food you have given us."

THE NEW MOON OF ID

The moon plays an important part in the Ramadan fast and festival of Id-ul-Fitr. The Muslim calendar is a lunar calendar in which the appearance of the moon shows when months begin and end. The new moon marks the beginning of a new month. As the new moon appears at the end of the month of Ramadan, the month of Shawwal begins. The festival of Id-ul-Fitr starts at this time.

The moon and stars have long been important in the Muslim calendar. When Muhammad ﷺ lived, people knew the date by carefully recording the cycles of the moon. People would often travel by night using the moon to light their way and the stars to decide which direction to travel.

This mosque in Abu Dhabi is lit up at the festival of Id-ul-Fitr.

Nobody is sure exactly when the new moon will come. Some months have thirty days and some are only twenty-nine days long. So during Ramadan, people try and work out what day the new moon will appear. The new moon appears at different times in different countries. In some Muslim countries, people climb to the top of the highest towers in the mosques or the highest hill or tree to see if the new moon will appear that night. If the night is cloudy, it is impossible to see if there is a new moon, and everybody becomes very anxious in case they have missed Id-ul-Fitr!

There is a crescent moon once Id has begun.

A GUIDING LIGHT

During the summer months when desert temperatures soar during the day, people often choose the night to travel across a desert when it is much cooler. In places where there are no roads, they still use the light of the moon to travel and use the stars to navigate the way, just as the Prophet Muhammad ﷺ did.

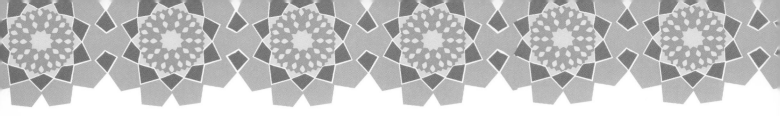

Officially, Id-ul-Fitr begins when the new moon is sighted in Mecca, the center of the Muslim faith. Religious officials in Mecca feel it is important that all Muslims celebrate Id-ul-Fitr together. As soon as the new moon is sighted, it is announced on the radio and this information is also sent by telephone or cable to every mosque and Saudi embassy in the world. Muslims living in non-Muslim countries ring up the Saudi Arabian Embassy or a local mosque to see if Id has arrived. There is also an Id telephone helpline in Mecca that people can call to see if the new moon has arrived.

People have mixed feelings about the arrival of Id. Many religious people feel sad that the Ramadan fast is ending because that is the time that they feel closest to God. Children are excited because presents are always given at Id. For parents the end of Ramadan is a busy time. They have to do their religious duties but at the same time they have to do lots of shopping for Id presents and for special festive food. In Muslim countries the stores always stay open all night in the last weeks of Ramadan in preparation for Id.

THE MUSLIM CALENDAR

The Muslim calendar is called the Hegira (Hijra), which means "migration" in Arabic. The Muslim calendar starts from the time of one of the most important events of the history of Islam. In 622 CE the Prophet Muhammad ﷺ and his followers were forced to leave Mecca and live in the city of Medina, where Islam became a major religion.

The Muslim Hijra calendar has 12 months. Each Muslim month lasts from one full moon to the next and this means months can be either 29 or 30 days long. A Muslim year has approximately 354 days, so is about 11 days shorter than the year of 365 days. It also means that festivals such as Id-ul-Fitr will appear about 11 days earlier each year. So if Id-ul-Fitr is celebrated on February 8 in 1997 it will be celebrated 11 days earlier in 1998, depending on when the moon arrives and how long the months in between are!

In Mecca, the center of the Muslim world, Muslims wait to see the appearance of the new moon over Mecca to officially begin the Id-ul-Fitr celebrations.

ISLAMIC CALENDAR

MUHARRAM
Al-Hegira
SAFAR
RABI-UL-AWWAL
Meelad-ul-Nabal
RABI-UL-AKHIR
JAMADA-AL-AWWAL
JAMADA-ALAKHIR
RAJAB
Lailat-ul-Isra
SHA'BAN
Lailat-ul-Barh
RAMADAN
Lailat-ul-Quadr
SHAWWAL
Id-ul-Fitr
DHUL-QA'ADDA
DHUL-HIJJAH
Id-ul-Adha

See pages 28–29 for more information on these festivals.

ID BEGINS WITH PRAYERS

At first light the loud, musical voice of the muezzin breaks the silence of the night as he summons Muslims to prayer.

Id-ul-Fitr is a time for celebrating, but Allah always comes first. Before the presents are opened and the food is eaten, all Muslims go to the mosque for prayers.

Prayer is important to Muslims. Muslims pray five times a day but do not always go to the mosque for prayers. Muhammad ﷺ felt that the whole world was God's mosque and he told Muslims they could say their prayers anywhere as long as it was clean. Everybody has the same times for prayer, as laid out in the scriptures, but not all Muslims pray at the same time as time changes around the world. On Fridays and special occasions such as Id-ul-Fitr, Muslims go to the mosque for prayer.

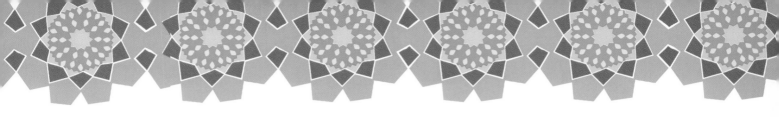

Muslims are called to the mosque for prayer. Mosques have tall towers called minarets and traditionally, a person called a muezzin, who has a loud, clear voice, climbs to the top of the minaret and recites the call to prayer, which is called the adhan. In the morning, Muslims get up at dawn, called by the sound of the muezzin's musical voice ringing out from the mosque, and go to the mosque still feeling sleepy.

Today, many mosques use loudspeakers to call Muslims to the mosque. When the call from the mosque cannot be heard, Muslims have to wake themselves up and go to the mosque, where the call to prayer is said from a platform inside.

Muslim women come in to pray at a mosque in India. Women pray in a separate part of the mosque to Muslim men. If a mosque is not big enough to have a separate area for women, they pray at home.

These are the words of the adhan, or call to prayer, that the muezzin will say to gather Muslims to the mosque.

God is great! God is great!
God is great! God is great!
I bear witness that there is no God but Allah.
I bear witness that there is no God but Allah.
I bear witness that Muhammad ﷺ is the messenger of God.
I bear witness that Muhammad ﷺ is the messenger of God.
Come to prayer! Come to prayer!
Come to salvation! Come to salvation!
God is great! God is great!
There is no God but Allah.
(At dawn the following is added)
Prayer is better than sleep! Prayer is better than sleep!

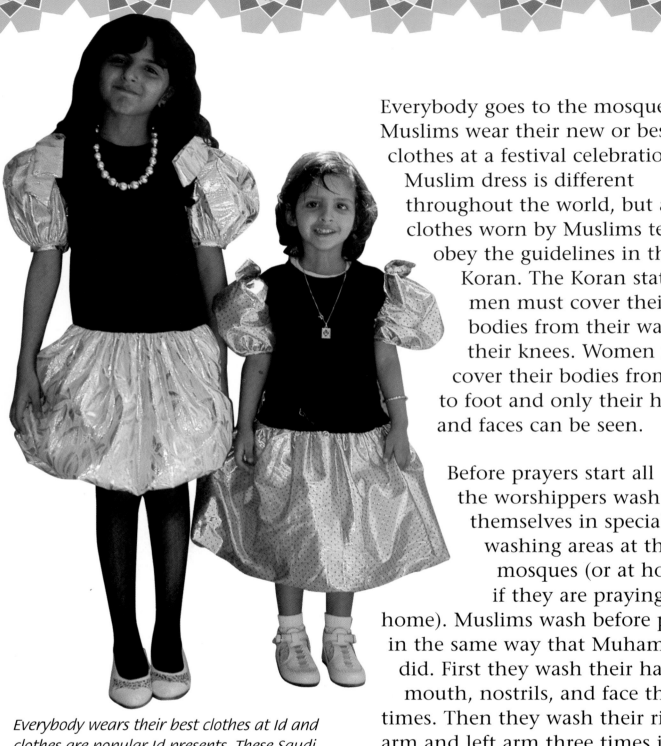

Everybody goes to the mosque at Id. Muslims wear their new or best clothes at a festival celebration. Muslim dress is different throughout the world, but all the clothes worn by Muslims tend to obey the guidelines in the Koran. The Koran states that men must cover their bodies from their waist to their knees. Women must cover their bodies from head to foot and only their hands and faces can be seen.

Before prayers start all the worshippers wash themselves in special washing areas at the mosques (or at home, if they are praying at home). Muslims wash before prayers in the same way that Muhammad ﷺ did. First they wash their hands, mouth, nostrils, and face three times. Then they wash their right arm and left arm three times in that order. Finally they wash their head, ears, neck, and feet three times.

Everybody wears their best clothes at Id and clothes are popular Id presents. These Saudi children posing in their new Id party clothes do not have to dress according to Islamic laws until they are older. In a few years' time they will have to wear long robes and a veil.

These Muslims are praying on colorful rugs and prayer mats in a mosque in Cairo, Egypt. Muslims have to use different positions during prayer and these young worshippers are still learning what to do.

It is important to make sure that the ground Muslims are praying on is clean, even in a mosque. Most Muslims do this by using a prayer mat, but those who cannot afford one use a clean cloth. There are special positions to use when praying and everyone faces Mecca when they are at prayer.

Following the rules of the Koran, Muslims always wash in running water before they pray in a mosque.

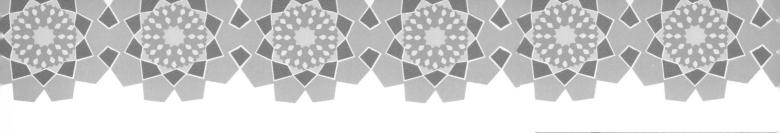

A prayer leader called an Imam always leads Id prayers. There are special prayers that are always said at Id and there is always a sermon.

After the prayers everybody exchanges traditional Id Mubarak (Happy Id) greetings, and a festive atmosphere overtakes the mosque. In the courtyard of the mosque, or just outside the mosque, there are always food stalls. Everybody spends time at the mosque with friends before going home for presents and family celebrations. In non-Muslim countries, Muslims might travel long distances to reach the mosque and they might spend the day at the mosque meeting old friends and making new ones.

Above: Many people travel long distances to join in the Id celebrations at large mosques in towns and cities. The food stalls around the mosque mean that worshippers can share an Id feast together.

Left: Muslims of different nationalities exchange Id Mubarak greetings at Regent's Park Mosque, London.

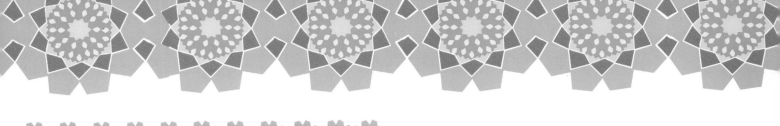

A VISIT TO A CEMETERY

Id is a time for family. It is a time when Muslims also remember members of their family who have died. Most families visit the graves of dead relatives at Id.

Muslims believe they only go to Paradise if Allah allows them to—nobody is assured of a life after death. Only people who give up their lives fighting in a just cause for Islam are assured of entering Paradise.

Large mosques in European and American cities are always colorful at Id-ul-Fitr. Muslims from all over the world visit the mosques dressed in their national costumes.

All Muslims learn Arabic so that they can read the Koran, and use Arabic to talk to new friends from different countries at large Id gatherings.

A Muslim cemetery in Morocco. All the headstones face the same way because all Muslims are buried with their heads toward Mecca.

GIVING TO OTHERS

Before Muslims leave the mosque at Id, they have to give a special welfare payment to the mosque called the zakat-ul-Fitr. Everybody has to give zakat-ul-Fitr and the giving of the zakat is seen by most Muslims as an act of worship.

The Prophet Muhammad ﷺ wanted everybody to feast at Id, including poor people who could not normally afford a good meal. The amount of zakat-ul-Fitr people have to pay is set every year and is always the cost of a meal. Rich people often give much more than this. In some countries people might give the cost of a meal in actual foodstuffs but in most places the zakat is given in cash. This means that the mosque has enough money or food to provide a festive meal for the poor. Muslims living in non-Muslim countries will pay their zakat-ul-Fitr early so it can be sent out to a poor country via the mosque or an Islamic welfare organization.

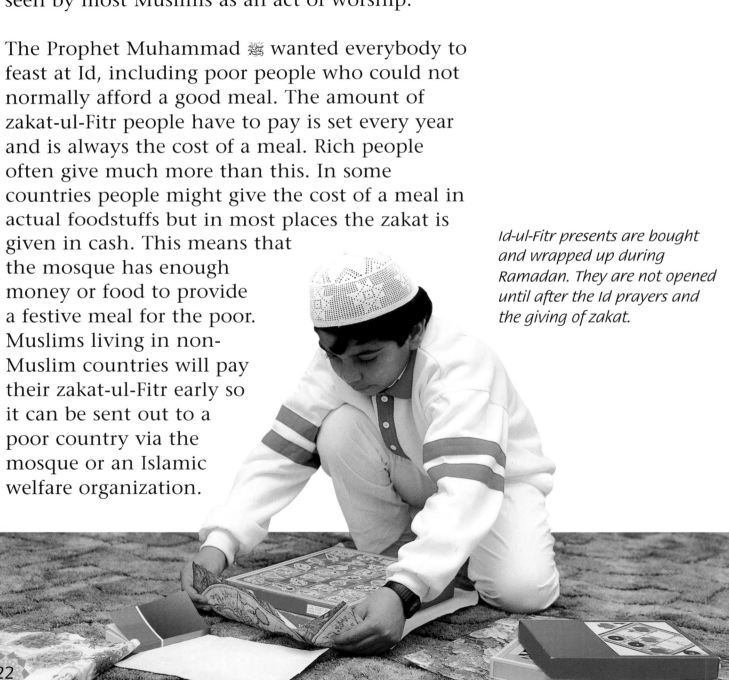

Id-ul-Fitr presents are bought and wrapped up during Ramadan. They are not opened until after the Id prayers and the giving of zakat.

ID CARDS

Everybody sends their family and friends Id Mubarak cards at Id. Most cards are decorated with quotations from the Koran beautifully written by skilled Muslim calligraphers. Islamic calligraphy has become an art form and calligraphers use ink, gold dust, and gems to form letters and make colorful borders around the writing. Verses from the Koran are also written in a special way to form different shapes such as minarets.

Left: Children open their cards at Id. The card on the floor has Arabic writing made into a pattern.

Once the zakat is given everybody is free to return home for presents. Clothes, candy, and toys are popular presents for children at Id.

Chinese Muslims giving zakat at a mosque. Children have to pay zakat as well as adults and are expected to save their money so that they can afford to pay the zakat.

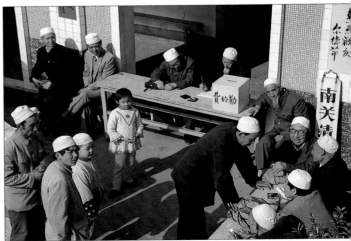

CELEBRATIONS

The festival of Id-ul-Fitr is a family celebration. In countries in the Muslim world it is a three-day festival, but Muslims living in non-Islamic countries often have to go to work or school and are only able to celebrate for one day.

Muslims around the world celebrate Id-ul-Fitr by eating rich, festive food. Every country has its own special Id recipes. All these recipes follow the guidelines about food in the Koran. Muslims can only eat meat that is killed in a special way and is halal, or "allowed." They are forbidden to eat pork. The drinking of alcoholic beverages such as wine, beer, and spirits is also forbidden.

Children with a traditional Indian or Pakistani meal of pakoras: lamb cooked in a spicy hot sauce with rice and a dessert.

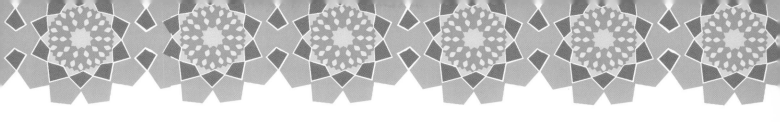

Other celebrations vary around the world. In the Middle East and north Africa horse racing is popular. All over the UAE (United Arab Emirates) a favorite outing is a day at the races. Members of the royal family, who own race horses, spend the day watching their horses from richly embroidered tents. Camel races in Morocco are less formal and proud owners of camels travel for long distances to enter their camels in the Id races.

Another popular Id sport in the north of Iran, Turkmenistan, Pakistan, Afghanistan, and an area of Turkey and Iraq known as Kurdistan is traditional tribal polo. This is an exciting experience. Bearded tribesmen wearing colorful clothes and mounted on tough, shaggy ponies challenge nearby tribes or villages to a polo match. A rough playing field is marked out with goals at either end and teams try to hit a ball or a goat's skull into their opponent's goal.

Children in Pakistan dress in their best clothes to watch the polo matches. The girls cover their heads and wear the salwar kameez, a loose tunic worn over baggy trousers.

A street procession to celebrate Id in Nigeria. Festivals are colorful occasions in Africa with the men wearing long robes and turbans.

In countries such as India and Turkey there are festive markets with vendors selling candies, jewelry, and other interesting things. Acrobats and groups of actors or even amusement parks are part of these markets. In Africa there is traditional singing.

Dancing is forbidden in the Koran, so orthodox Muslims do not dance as part of their celebration. However, a few different nationalities do dance at Id. The dances are often ancient dances that were danced before conversion to Islam. Some African peoples express their strong religious feelings by dancing in a trance, and are a colorful sight as they whirl around and around.

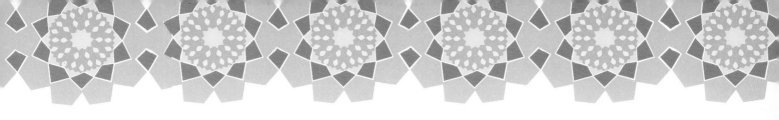

Camel racing in Saudi Arabia. Camels are popular animals in desert countries such as Saudi Arabia, because they can travel easily across the sand and can go for many days without food or water. The Prophet Muhammad ﷺ used to lead camel trains across the desert carrying goods to trade in different towns and cities.

The Koran is often at the center of Id celebrations. In Malaysia and East Africa there are Koran reciting competitions. It is considered a great achievement to be able to recite the Koran by memory and many people are able to do this. Others are able to recite the poetry of the Koran in beautiful ways. The winners of these Koran reciting competitions will certainly be given the honor of being invited to read from the Koran throughout the next year's Ramadan and Id celebrations.

OTHER MUSLIM FESTIVALS

In Islam there are six annual celebrations. There are the two festivals which were introduced by the Prophet Muhammad ﷺ, Id-ul-Fitr and Id-ul-Adha. The other four celebrations remember events that took place in the Prophet's life.

Al-Hegira
The 1st of Muharram is the first day of the New Year, New Year's Day. It is also the time when Muslims remember the Hegira, or migration of the Prophet Muhammad ﷺ and his followers from Mecca to Medina.

On New Year's day Muslims exchange new year greetings and meet in groups to tell stories of how the Prophet and his followers fled from Mecca to Medina.

Meelad-ul-Nabal
The Prophet Muhammad ﷺ was born on the 12th day of Rabi-ul-Awwal, which is known as the month of the birth.

▼ Muslims meet in groups on this day

to relate stories from the life of the Prophet Muhammad ﷺ. It is also a time when Muslims think about how they can follow the example that the Prophet set in his daily life.

Lailat-ul-Isra (The Night of the Journey)
According to Chapter 17 of the Koran, the angel, Gabriel, mounted on a winged horse called Buraq, took the Prophet Muhammad ﷺ on a night journey to Heaven. There he met the prophets, including Abraham, Moses, and Jesus. Allah also instructed him to make his followers pray five times a day. This event took place on the 27th night of Rajab. Muslims remember this event by saying additional prayers.

Laila-ul-Barh (The Night of Forgiveness)
Two weeks before Ramadan begins, Muslims begin to prepare themselves spiritually for the fast by asking Allah to forgive their sins.

Ramadan is the month of the fast, when Muslims don't eat from dawn to sunset. This fast was established by the Prophet Muhammad ﷺ and recalls the time when the Koran was first recited to Muhammad ﷺ by the angel Gabriel. This event is said to have taken place on the Night of Power, the 27th night of Ramadan.

Id-ul-Fitr (The festival of the breaking of the fast)
This is one of the two festivals introduced by the Prophet Muhammad ﷺ that celebrates the end of the Ramadan fast.

Id-ul-Adha (The festival of the sacrifice)
This is the second festival introduced by the Prophet Muhammad ﷺ. This festival remembers the time when Abraham decided to sacrifice his son, Ishmael, to Allah and how Allah put a ram in Ishmael's place. To Muslims this is an example of how they must sacrifice everything they have for God and for Islam.

◄ Every Muslim who can afford it will go on a pilgrimage, or hajj, to Mecca. Everybody wants to do this at least once in their lifetime. In Mecca they visit the Kaaba, which was built by Abraham as a monument to Allah. Everybody has a special meal called the umra during the festival at which a roast sheep is eaten.

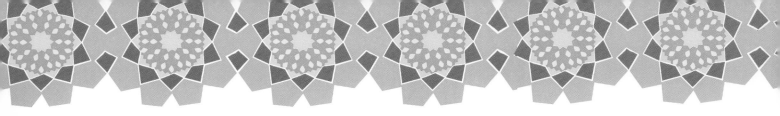

GLOSSARY

Abraham A prophet, the father of Ishmael and Isaac.

Allah The Arabic name for God. Muslims believe that there is only one God, Allah.

Calligraphy Writing as an art form.

Fast To give up eating and drinking. Muslims fast from dawn to sunset during Ramadan.

Imam A person who leads prayers in mosques and helps people to understand what is written in the Koran.

Islam The Muslim religion. Muslims believe that they must submit their lives to Allah in every way.

Kaaba A cube-shaped structure in the center of the grand mosque in Mecca.

Koran The name given to the Muslim's Holy Book.

Mecca A city in present-day Saudi Arabia. It houses the Kaaba, a monument to Allah, and is also the birthplace of the Prophet Muhammad ﷺ.

Medina A city in present-day Saudi Arabia. The Prophet Muhammad ﷺ lived in Medina during his exile from Mecca. Medina is the second most sacred city in Islam and is where the Prophet Muhammad ﷺ is buried.

Meditating Thinking deeply, usually about religion.

Minaret The name given to a tower in a mosque.

Mosque A place where Muslims go to worship.

Muslim A follower of Islam. Muslims believe in one God, Allah, and try to live their lives by doing exactly what God wants them to do.

Prophet A person chosen by Allah to instruct people as to the will of Allah. The Muslim prophets are the same as Christian and Hebrew prophets and include Jesus and Muhammad ﷺ.

Quraysh The tribe that the Prophet Muhammad ﷺ came from. Muslims believe that the twelve Arab tribes are descended from the twelve sons of Ishmael, the son of Abraham.

Scroll A long, rolled-up piece of paper, used before books were made.

Welfare organization
An organization or charity that gives money to poor people. The main Islamic welfare organization is called the Red Crescent.

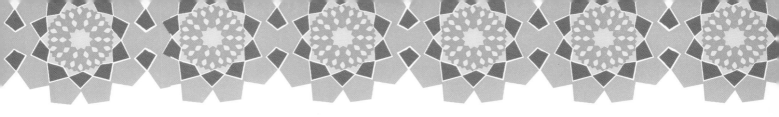

OTHER BOOKS ABOUT ID-UL-FITR

Kerven, Rosalind. *Id-ul-Fitr (World of Holidays)*. Chatham, NJ: Raintree Steck-Vaughn, 1997.

MacMillan, Dianne M. *Ramadan and Id-Al-Fitr (Best Holidays Books)*. Springfield, NJ: Enslow Pub, 1994.

Stone, Susheila. *Eid Ul-Fitr (Celebrations)*. New York: Talman, 1995.

FOR MORE INFORMATION

Information on Islamic Festivals - Muslim Celebrations
http://www10.geocities.com/Athens/1408/festival.htm

Commemoration & Celebration: Islamic Festivals in Singapore
http://irdu.nus.sg/kampungnet/beliefs.html

India (Goa) Picture of Mosque Where Festival is Celebrated
http://www.goa-interactive.com/goa/mosque.htm
http://www.royalperspective.com/Goa/Info/mosques.htm

Trinidad-Tobago
http://tidco.co.tt/arts/festival/festivals.html

Search or Browse the Koran On Line
http://www.hti.umich.edu/relig/koran

General Information, Beliefs, History of Islam, etc.
http://www.scit.wlv.ac.uk/~cm5223/islam/islam.html

Links to Various Islamic Internet Sites
http://www.irshad.org/pages/islsites.htm

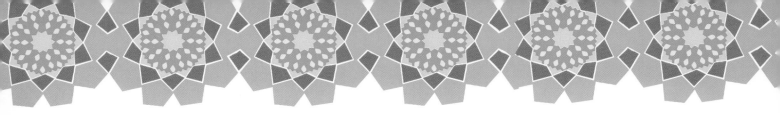

INDEX